Exploring Science

The Exploring Science series is designed to familiarize young students with science topics taught in grades 4–9. The topics in each book are divided into knowledge and understanding sections, followed by exploration by means of simple projects or experiments. The topics are also sequenced from easiest to more complex, and should be worked through until the correct level of attainment for the age and ability of the student is reached. Carefully planned Test Yourself questions at the end of each topic allow the student to gain a sense of achievement on mastering the subject.

EXPLORING
WEATHER

Ed Catherall

STECK-VAUGHN
LIBRARY
Austin, Texas

Exploring Science

Electricity
Energy Sources
Light
Magnets
Soil and Rocks
Sound
Uses of Energy
Weather

Cover illustrations:
Top A hang glider against the evening sky.
Below left A newspaper weather forecast map.
Below right Ice crystals formed on glass.

Frontispiece Vacationers enjoying the hot weather on Oahu, one of the Hawaiian Islands.

Editor: Elizabeth Spiers/Cally Chambers
Editor, American Edition: Susan Wilson
Series Designer: Ross George

Published in the United States in 1991 by Steck-Vaughn Co., Austin, Texas, a subsidiary of the National Education Corporation.

First published in 1990 by
Wayland (Publishers) Ltd

© Copyright 1990 Wayland (Publishers) Ltd

Library of Congress Cataloging-in-Publication Data

Catherall, Ed.
  Exploring weather / Ed Catherall.

    p.   cm.—(Exploring science)
      Includes bibliography references (p.) and index.
      Summary: Discusses such aspects of the weather as air currents, temperature, world weather patterns, air pollution, and climate and agriculture. Includes activities and experiments.
    ISBN 0-8114-2596-7
    1. Weather—Juvenile literature. [1. Weather.] I. Title.
  II. Series: Catherall, Ed. Exploring science.
  QC981.3.C38   1990   90-10025
  551.4—dc20   CIP
                                               AC

Typeset by Multifacit Graphics, Keyport, NJ
Printed in Italy by G. Canale, C.S.p.A., Turin
Bound in the United States by Lake Book Manufacturing, Inc., Melrose Park, IL.
    2 3 4 5 6 7 8 9 0 Ca 95 94 93 92

Contents

THE WEATHER AND PEOPLE

Weather affects the lives of people all over the world. The clothes we wear, what type of house we live in, and the food we eat all depend on our climate. The crops that we grow depend on the weather; too much rain causes floods, while too little rain results in droughts. It can also be too cold or too hot for seedling plants to thrive.

Weather, therefore, has always been vital to life. Over the years, people have tried to predict the weather and developed sayings, or weather lore, to help them. An example is the saying, "Red sky at night is the sailor's delight, red sky at morning is the sailor's warning." Most North American and European weather comes from the west. A red sky at night means that the sun setting in the west is shining onto clouds in the east. These clouds have passed and the clear sky means good weather is coming. A red sky at morning means that the sun rising in the east is reflecting onto clouds in the west. These clouds are approaching, bringing bad weather.

Another old saying with some truth in it is, "Rain before seven, dry before eleven." Usually, a weather front (see page 34) does take about four hours to pass over.

Plants and animals are used in weather lore. Take, for example, "Many berries on the holly means a cold winter." Actually, this is more likely to mean that there has been a good summer for the berries to form. Another dubious saying is, "Swallows fly low when cold weather is coming." Swallows feed on flying insects that cannot fly high in cold, windy weather, so swallows fly low when cold weather has actually arrived. In general, animals and plants cannot be used to predict weather.

According to weather lore, a red sky at night can mean that good weather is on the way.

ACTIVITY

HOW THE WEATHER AFFECTS US

YOU NEED

- **a collection of weather sayings**
- **a scrapbook**
- **a large sheet of paper**

1 Describe today's weather. Is the temperature in your room the same as the temperature outside? If not, why not? How is your room temperature controlled?
2 Are the clothes that you have on suitable to wear inside and outside? What do you think the weather will be like in 4 hours? Will your clothes be suitable then?
3 Read your collection of weather sayings. Do you think any are true?
4 Are there any sayings that are local to your area? Ask older people if they can remember some.
5 How could you test each of your weather sayings?
6 Start a scrapbook on weather. Include newspaper cuttings of the weather worldwide.
7 Use a large sheet of paper to start a weather chart.
8 Record the weather daily for a month. This book will help you to improve your observations.

Winters in Canada are extremely cold. These children in Ontario have to dress warmly to go to school.

TEST YOURSELF

1. Describe a natural disaster that was caused by the weather.
2. What would be ideal weather to grow crops in your district?
3. Find out about and describe the type of house that different people live in to cope with their climates.

AIR IS ALL AROUND US

The Earth is surrounded by an envelope of air called the atmosphere. It consists of different layers. The layer nearest the ground is called the troposphere. It is only 6 miles thick, which is not much higher than the top of Mount Everest. Near the equator, the troposphere is thicker; often more than 10 miles. This layer contains enough oxygen for us to breathe.

Above the troposphere is the stratosphere, which reaches a height of 30 miles above the Earth's surface. In this layer, the air does not contain enough oxygen for us to breathe properly. The temperature of -80°F is far too cold to hold any moisture, so there are no clouds here.

The atmosphere does more than provide us with our weather. It is essential to life on our planet. Apart from providing us with vital gases to breathe, it acts as a blanket, keeping out half the heat from the sun. A lot of the sun's harmful, ultraviolet rays are absorbed by ozone, a type of oxygen. The stratosphere contains quite a large amount of ozone in a layer between 12 and 22 miles above the ground.

The air blanket, with its clouds in the lowest layer, also helps keep the Earth warm at night and blocks the heat from the sun during the day. This stops the day and night temperatures from changing too much, which would threaten life. Clouds also contain water essential to life.

Below *The atmosphere is made up of five layers—the troposphere, stratosphere, mesosphere, thermosphere, and exosphere. The exosphere, above a height of about 300 miles, is where the atmosphere merges into interplanetary space.*

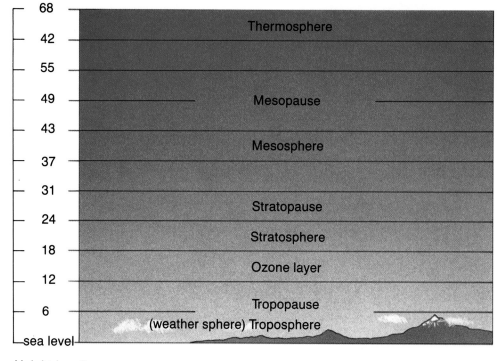

Height in miles	
68	
42	Thermosphere
55	
49	Mesopause
43	
37	Mesosphere
31	
24	Stratopause
18	Stratosphere
12	Ozone layer
6	Tropopause
	(weather sphere) Troposphere
sea level	

Height in miles

Less oxygen
in atmosphere

ACTIVITY

YOU NEED

- **a large plastic bowl**
- **water**
- **clear plastic or glass bottles**

1 Half fill the bowl with water.
2 Take an empty plastic or glass bottle.
3 Turn the bottle upside down. Plunge the neck straight down into the bowl of water. Does water go into the empty bottle?

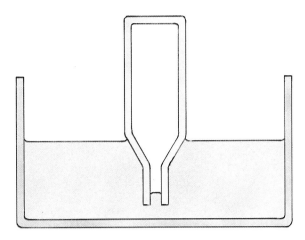

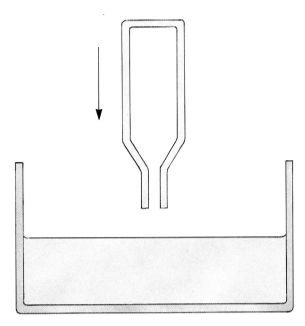

4 Push the bottle deeper into the water. What do you feel?

5 What happens if you let go of the bottle? Can you explain this?
6 Plunge the "empty" bottle, upside down, into the water again.
7 Turn the bottle, so that the neck turns slightly upward. What happens?

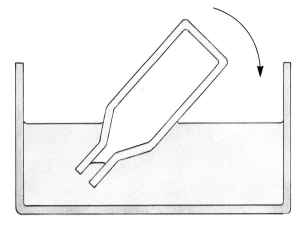

8 What comes out of your "empty" bottle? What is inside it?

TEST YOURSELF

1. What is the lowest layer of the atmosphere called? How thick is it?
2. Why are clouds found only in the lowest layer of the atmosphere?
3. Why is the atmosphere essential for life on Earth?

SUNSHINE AND TEMPERATURE

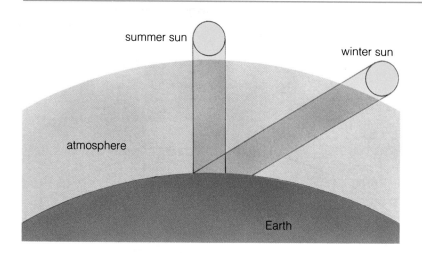

summer sun

winter sun

atmosphere

Earth

Temperatures are higher in summer than in winter. In summer the sun is more directly overhead and the rays are concentrated on the Earth's surface. In winter the sun is lower in the sky. Its rays have to travel a greater distance through the atmosphere, and they are less concentrated on the Earth's surface, so the weather is cooler.

Almost all the heat on Earth comes from the sun. When it is directly above a point on the Earth's surface, in the middle of the day, the sun's rays have the shortest journey through the atmosphere. Little heat is lost. As the Earth spins around, the distance that the sun's rays have to travel through the atmosphere to reach the same point increases, and the air gets cooler.

The Earth circles around the sun once a year. The axis around which the Earth spins (once every 24 hours) is tilted. Because of this the seasons vary in different parts of the world. When the sun is overhead at noon on the Tropic of Cancer, it is

the summer solstice in the northern hemisphere and the winter solstice in the southern hemisphere. Six months later, when the sun is overhead at noon on the Tropic of Capricorn, it is the winter solstice in the northern hemisphere and the summer solstice in the south.

The Earth is curved, so the sun's rays always have farther to travel through the atmosphere over the poles than anywhere else in the world. The sun's rays always have the shortest distance to travel over the equator. The temperature decreases from the equator to the poles. The equator is always hot, and the poles always cold.

WHAT IS THE TEMPERATURE TODAY?

YOU NEED

- **a thermometer**
- **a sunny day**

1 Measure the temperature on the ground in the sun and in the shade.

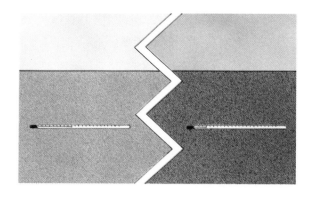

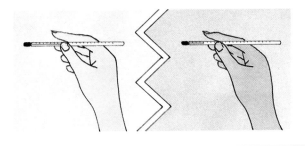

2 Measure the temperature of the air in the sun and in the shade.
3 How does the air temperature compare with the ground temperature?
4 Record these temperatures every hour throughout the day. Which was the hottest hour? Explain.

TEMPERATURES AROUND THE WORLD

1 Hold the sheet of paper vertically in front of the flashlight. What shape is the spot of light on the paper?

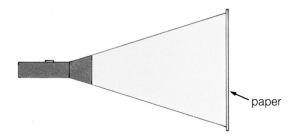

paper

2 Tilt the paper slightly. What happens to the light?
3 Compare how far the light travels to the center of the paper and to its edges. If the light were the sun, which part of the paper would be hottest and which coldest?

4 Find where you live on the globe of the world.
5 Hold your flashlight over the Tropic of Cancer and shine it onto the place where you live. Notice what happens to the spot of light.

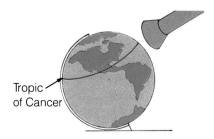

Tropic of Cancer

6 Now shine the flashlight on the equator. How is this different?

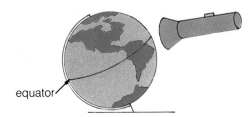

equator

7 Shine the flashlight on the Tropic of Capricorn. What happens to the spot of light? Where is the sun when it is the summer solstice for you?

TEST YOURSELF

1. Where does the Earth's heat come from?
2. Where is the sun at the time of the winter solstice?
3. Explain why it is hotter at the equator than at the poles.

AIR CURRENTS

When the sun shines on the Earth, part of the sun's energy, in the form of heat, is absorbed by the Earth. The land heats up faster than the sea, because the sea moves constantly. Air that is in contact with the land heats up faster than air over the sea.

When air is heated, it expands, taking up more space. The air particles move farther apart, so the air becomes thinner and lighter; we say it is at low pressure. Because of this, the heated air rises above the surrounding air. This is called a thermal air current. You can often see gliders or birds circling around in rising air currents.

The Earth spins from east to west, and this spin affects the movement of the air. In the northern hemisphere, a region of rising warm air spins in a counterclockwise direction. This area of spinning low pressure air is also called a depression or a cyclone. A hurricane is a large tropical cyclone.

The warm air rises and gets cooler as it leaves the Earth's surface. Eventually, it becomes cold air. The particles in the air move closer together as the air cools. The air contracts, takes up less space, and becomes denser and heavier. This air is at high pressure. As it sinks down toward the Earth, the high-pressure air flows into the

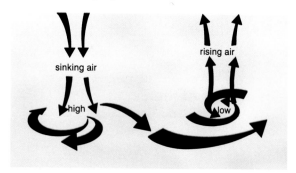

sinking air

rising air

high

low

depression. This is spinning counterclockwise, so the high-pressure, cold anticyclone spins clockwise as its air rushes into the depression. A depression spins clockwise and an anticyclone spins counter clockwise.

ACTIVITIES

HOT AIR RISES

YOU NEED

- **a circular plate**
- **aluminum foil**
- **a pair of scissors**
- **thread**
- **an electric toaster**

WARNING: Be careful with electric toasters. Ask an adult to help you.

Hang gliders make use of rising air currents to lift them higher into the sky.

1 Place the plate on the aluminum foil and trace it. Cut out the circle.

2 Draw a spiral in the circle, about ¾ in wide and cut it out.

3 Make a small hole in the middle of the spiral. Tie thread to the hole so that the spiral can be hung up.

4 Hold the spiral over an electric toaster that is turned off.

5 Turn on the toaster. What happens to the spiral? As the toaster heats up, do not let the hot air burn you.

LAND HEATS UP FASTER THAN THE SEA

YOU NEED

- **2 identical large plastic tubs**
- **dry soil with the stones removed**
- **water**
- **2 thermometers**
- **a sunny day**

1 Fill one tub with dry soil. Fill the other tub with water.

2 Carefully put a thermometer into each tub. Record the temperature of the soil and the water.

3 Place both tubs in the sun.

4 Record each temperature again after 30 minutes. Which heated faster?

5 Record each temperature in another 30 minutes.

	Start	after 30 mins.	after 1 hour
Temperature of soil (°F)			
Temperature of water (°F)			

6 Put both tubs in the shade. Which cools faster—the soil or the water?

TEST YOURSELF

1. Why does a thermal air current rise?
2. In which direction does a cyclone spin in the northern hemisphere?
3. Why does cool air have a higher pressure than warm air?

WORLD WEATHER PATTERNS

Air rises over the hot equator and sinks over the cold polar regions. This creates a band of low pressure at the equator and high pressure over the poles. There are three main systems of winds between the poles and the equator. The polar easterlies blow from the poles toward the temperate regions; the westerlies blow away from the tropics toward the temperate zones; and the trade winds blow from the tropics toward the equator.

SEA BREEZES

On an island in summer, the sun heats the land and it becomes hotter than the sea. Hot air rises over the land. Cool air is drawn in from the sea to replace the rising hot air. This creates an onshore (moving inland) sea breeze. The rising hot air is pulled over the sea to replace the air drawn onto the land. This air gets cold and sinks, completing the wind cycle. As the land cools at night, the sea stays warmer than the land. Warm air rises from the sea. Cool air is drawn from the land to replace this rising air, creating an offshore wind.

Above *During the day warm air rises over land and draws in a cool onshore breeze.*
Below *At night warm air rises over the sea causing a cool offshore breeze.*

ACTIVITY

1 Find the equator on the globe. Which major cities are near the equator?
2 Find the 30° and 60° latitudes. The temperate zone is between these two lines. Which major cities are near these latitudes?

3 Look in the newspaper for major city temperatures. What were the temperatures for these cities? Where are they? How do they compare with the area in which you live?
4 Look in the atlas for wind patterns. Some famous winds are the doldrums at the equator, the westerlies, and the trade winds. Notice that the westerlies are called the "roaring forties" in the southern hemisphere.
5 Look in the atlas for the major ocean currents. Compare them with the wind patterns. What do you notice?

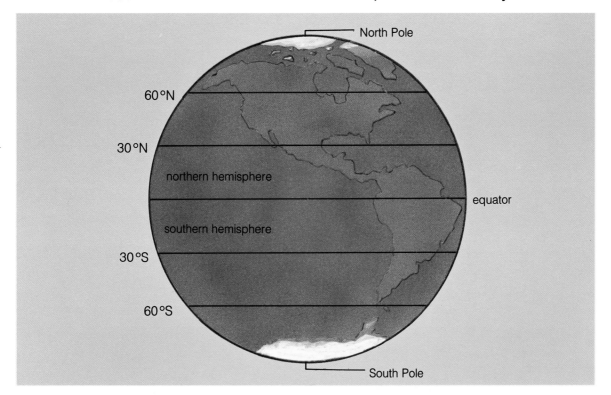

TEST YOURSELF

1. Which winds blow from the tropics toward the equator?
2. Draw a map of the Earth and mark the world's main wind systems.
3. Describe how sea breezes blow on an island.

THE WIND

Wherever you live, the wind comes from one main direction and is called the prevailing wind. It is caused by the world wind patterns (see page 14). However, this general direction can change, depending on the air currents at the time and whether the wind in these currents is moving in a clockwise or counterclockwise direction. Variations are also caused by large areas of water, such as oceans and lakes (see page 14). Hills and mountains divert the wind upward, over them, and then down the other side. Valleys channel the wind. Buildings and tall trees act as windbreaks, or cause the wind to swirl, just as the tide swirls around a rock on the beach.

In 1805, Sir Francis Beaufort, an Englishman, devised the Beaufort scale to estimate wind speeds. This system measures the general wind speed over ten minutes, ignoring the gusts.

Above Mountain ranges, such as the Southern Alps in New Zealand, affect wind direction, diverting winds up and over them.

Beaufort scale		Wind speed (mph)	Signs to look for
0	Calm	0–1	Smoke rises up
1	Light air	1–3	Smoke drifts
2	Light breeze	4–7	Leaves move; wind just felt on face
3	Gentle breeze	8–12	Leaves move constantly
4	Moderate breeze	13–18	Small branches move; flags flap
5	Fresh breeze	19–24	Small leafy trees sway
6	Strong breeze	25–31	Large branches move
7	Near gale	32–38	Whole trees sway
8	Fresh gale	39–46	Twigs break off trees
9	Strong gale	47–54	Large branches break off; house damage
10	Storm	55–63	Trees uprooted; major house damage
11	Violent storm	64–72	Widespread damage
12	Hurricane	73 +	Disaster

Wind-speed scale	
Angle	mph
90°	0
85°	5½
80°	8
70°	11¾
60°	15
50°	18
40°	21
35°	23½
30°	26
25°	28½
20°	32¼

ACTIVITY

WIND SPEED

YOU NEED

- **a thread**
- **a ping-pong ball**
- **cellophane tape**
- **a protractor**
- **a small spirit level**
- **a plastic bag**
- **a windy day**

1 Tape a length of thread to the ping-pong ball.
2 Tape the other end of the thread to the midpoint of the protractor. Check that the ball swings freely.
3 Tape the spirit level to the side of the protractor. You have made an anemometer (wind-speed meter).

4 Cut the bottom off the plastic bag.
5 Hold your plastic bag above your head. Hold it open. See which way it turns. This is the wind direction.

6 Hold your anemometer in the wind. Go into the open, away from trees and buildings, to do this.
7 Point the spirit level in the direction from which the wind is coming.

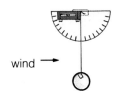

wind →

8 Check that the spirit-level bubble is in the center.
9 Ask a friend to read out the angle that the ball and thread make when the wind blows.

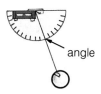

angle

10 Calculate the wind speed from the chart on page 16.
11 Record the average wind speed by taking ten readings in ten minutes.
12 Use the Beaufort scale on the opposite page to measure wind speed. Look for the signs given for the wind speeds in your record.

TEST YOURSELF

1. What does prevailing wind mean?
2. What can alter the direction of the prevailing wind?
3. What is the Beaufort scale?

WATER IN THE AIR

As saturated air cools and moisture condenses, fogs and mists may form, especially where the air is still.

Dry air absorbs (takes up) water through evaporation. Any water that is open to dry air will evaporate. Large quantities of water are absorbed from the sea, lakes, ponds, rivers, puddles, and streams. Plants and trees give off water; so does damp earth.

Evaporated water is held in the air as invisible water vapor. The amount of water vapor that the air will hold depends on its temperature. Hot air can hold more water than cold air. However, there is a maximum amount of water vapor that air can hold at a particular temperature. For example, air at 82°F can hold slightly less water than air at 85°F. We say that the air is saturated when it will not absorb any more water vapor. When the air is saturated, your clothes feel damp.

The comparison of the actual amount of water vapor in the air to the amount of water vapor in saturated air is called the relative humidity. When the air is saturated, the relative humidity is 100 percent.

Often air is not saturated—it holds less water than it can. If there is half the amount of water vapor in the air, the humidity is halved, or 50 percent.

When the saturated air cools down, it loses some of its water vapor. This invisible water vapor condenses (turns into water). Tiny droplets of water appear in the air, and elsewhere, when this happens.

ACTIVITIES

AIR "DRIES UP" WATER

YOU NEED

- **a saucer**
- **a bowl**
- **a cup**
- **water**
- **a graduated cylinder**
- **a sunny day**

1 Use the graduated cylinder to put the same quantity of water into each of the three containers.

3 Which container has the largest water surface?
4 Look at the water in each container after 1 hour.
5 Pour the water back into the cylinder. How much is left?

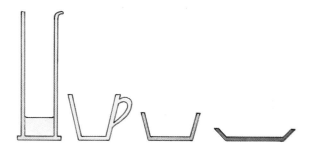

2 Put the containers on the window sill, or outside.

6 Repeat this for the saucer and bowl.
7 Compare the amount of water lost to the size of the water surface. Is there a pattern to your results?

SATURATED AIR

YOU NEED

- **2 identical small saucers**
- **a graduated cylinder**
- **water**
- **a plastic tub that will cover one saucer**

1 Use the cylinder to put the same quantity of water into both saucers.
2 Put them in the shade and cover one with the tub.

3 After 1 hour, measure the amount of water in both saucers.
4 Which saucer has had more water evaporated from it?
5 Look in the plastic tub. Is there any water sticking to its sides? The tub traps the air over the saucer and this air becomes saturated.

TEST YOURSELF

1. Which holds more water vapor—warm air or cool air?
2. What is relative humidity?
3. What happens when saturated air is cooled?

FROST, MIST, AND FOG

Water can be found in three forms—solid (ice), liquid (water), and gas (water vapor). Warm air contains water vapor (see page 18). Even if warm air is not saturated it still contains a lot of water vapor. As the temperature falls, the air becomes more humid, until it becomes saturated. If the air cools further, some of the water vapor condenses out, making water droplets. The temperature at which the water vapor condenses is called the dew point.

If the dew point is below the freezing point, 32°F, the water will condense out in the form of ice crystals, covering everything in frost. This usually happens on clear, cold nights, when the ground loses heat rapidly. The air in contact with the ground is cooled. In temperate lands, this happens in winter, early spring, and late autumn.

Fog and mist form when warm, moist air comes in contact with cold ground. As the ground cools at night, fog forms where the air is saturated, over rivers, lakes, and ponds. Freezing fog is formed when water droplets are at 32°F or lower. These "supercooled" droplets will remain liquid until they touch a cold surface and turn to ice.

Smog is a concentration of fog and smoke, usually occurring in large cities.

Above *Water vapor can condense into droplets on something as fine as a spider's web.*

Left *Frost on the edge of this maple leaf formed when the dew point was below freezing (32°F) and water condensed into ice crystals.*

ACTIVITY

CONDENSATION

> **YOU NEED**
>
> - **a refrigerator**
> - **a dry metal can**
> - **a bottle**
> - **ice cubes**
> - **a clean glass**
> - **a mirror**
> - **a large glass jar**

1 Clean the mirror and the glass.
2 Put them in the refrigerator for ten minutes.
3 Take out the mirror. Breathe on it. What do you see?

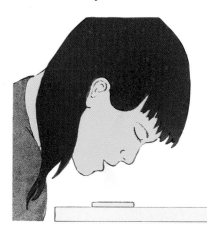

4 Take out the glass. Stand it on a table. What happens when the glass warms up?

5 Put ice cubes in the dry can. Watch the can's outside. What appears?

6 Fill the clean bottle with warm water from the tap. Set the bottle aside for several minutes. Pour out the water.
7 Stand a large ice cube on the top of the bottle. Can you see a cloud forming in the air just under the ice cube?

> **TEST YOURSELF**
>
> 1. What is the dew point?
> 2. Describe how frost forms.
> 3. How does fog form? What turns it into smog?

CLOUDS

Clouds are formed when saturated air cools. The excess water condenses out as tiny droplets of water. These droplets collide with others and get larger and heavier, until they fall as rain. Clouds can form when warm, moist air is carried into the upper atmosphere where it is colder. Clouds also form when saturated air is forced up over the top of a mountain. That is why mountains often have cloud cover.

There are three basic types of cloud. The highest are made of tiny ice crystals and are called cirrus. These wispy clouds are often followed by lower layers of stratus. These are light-gray sheets of cloud. They are composed of fine water droplets that become larger and larger as they collide with each other. There are three layers of stratus cloud: altostratus, nimbostratus, and the lowest layer, stratus.

The third kind of cloud is cumulus. These look like white, fluffy cauliflowers with a flat base. They are caused by an uprush of air. If the uprush is violent, the cloud will develop into the storm cloud cumulonimbus, which is dark and gives lightning, thunder, and rain.

There are all sorts of cloud combinations. Basically, white clouds are made of ice crystals. Light-gray clouds have small droplets that get bigger as the cloud gets darker and blacker, until it rains.

Above *Cirrus are very high, wispy clouds made up of feathery ice crystals.*

Below *This is often called a "mackerel sky" because the ripples of cloud look like fish scales. These cirrocumulus clouds bring unsettled weather.*

Below *Low, stormy nimbostratus clouds bring heavy rain or snow.*

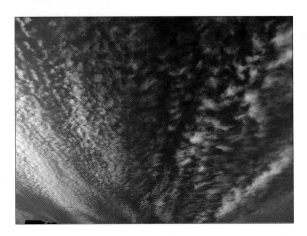

Above *Clusters of small, white cumulus clouds are usually a sign of fair weather.*

ACTIVITY

A CLOUD DISPLAY

> YOU NEED
>
> - **pictures of clouds**

1 Identify your cloud pictures.

2 Find out all you can about each cloud. Record this information in your own words.
3 Display your pictures with the information about them.
4 Record the clouds and the weather that you see every day. Record the time that you saw each cloud. Record the wind direction and how the cloud types changed.

TEST YOURSELF

1. Why are clouds often seen on the tops of mountains?
2. What are the three basic types of cloud?
3. Which cloud gives thunder and lightning?

RAIN

Rain forms in two ways. In the tropics, warm clouds rise, cool, and their water droplets condense. These liquid droplets collide with others, getting larger and larger, until the drops break up into smaller ones. Each of these then grows larger by colliding with others. When they move to cooler air, these drops fall as rain.

In cooler, temperate regions, the temperature of the cloud may drop to the freezing point or lower. This makes the tiny water droplets freeze. Any surrounding water vapor condenses onto the frozen droplets. These get larger and heavier eventually dropping to earth. As they fall, they get warmer, melt, and become raindrops.

There are three types of rainfall: convection, relief, and frontal (cyclonic). Convection rain is caused by heat. Hot air rises and cools, causing the water vapor to condense and fall as rain. This causes showers in temperate regions, or very heavy rain in the tropics.

Relief rain occurs when air is blown up over mountains and hills. As warm air rises up the side of a mountain, it cools, becomes saturated, and releases moisture as rain. Because the air has already released its moisture on the windward side, the far side of the mountain is dry. This is the "rain shadow."

The third kind of rain, frontal, is due to the changes in temperature caused by the advance of weather fronts (see page 34).

As saturated air rises over mountains and the temperature drops with altitude, the water vapor condenses and falls as relief rain.

ACTIVITY

MAKING A RAIN GAUGE

YOU NEED

- **a straight-sided glass jar**
- **cellophane tape**
- **a plastic funnel that fits in the glass jar**
- **a ruler**
- **modeling clay**

1 Use your ruler to draw marks every ¹/₈ inch on a piece of paper.
2 Tape this scale on the outside of the jar. Start the scale above the thickness of the bottom of the jar. Tape the scale facing inward so that you can read it through the jar.

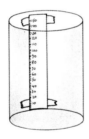

3 Place the funnel in the top of the jar.
4 Make sure it is fixed and watertight by putting a layer of modeling clay between the jar and the funnel.

5 Pour water in the funnel and practice reading different water levels.

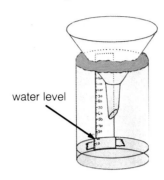

water level

6 Take off the funnel and clay, empty the jar, and dry it with a cloth.
7 Replace the funnel and clay.
8 Place your rain gauge outside to collect rainwater.
9 Record the depth of rain in your rain gauge each day.
10 Remember to empty your rain gauge each day.
11 Record your results as a bar graph.

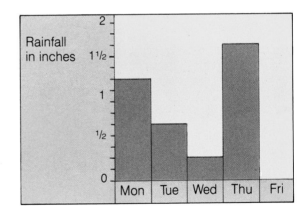

Rainfall in inches

TEST YOURSELF

1. How is rain formed in temperate regions?
2. What is convection rain?
3. What is relief rain? Give an example of where you might expect this rain to fall.

SNOW AND HAIL

Snow forms when tiny droplets of water condense and freeze into ice crystals. Then, more ice crystals freeze onto the original crystals. Many crystals have to be joined together to form a snowflake. If the air is very cold, the snowflake will be small, giving dry, powdery snow. This type of snow can be cleared by a snow blower.

If the air temperature is below 39°F, snow can fall, but it will only make wet, melting snow at the higher temperatures. At really freezing temperatures, the air is very dry. Snow may reach the ground from air at a temperature as high as 44°F, but it melts at once.

The air currents inside a large, towering cumulonimbus cloud are very strong and rise and fall. A falling raindrop can be carried up to the top of the cloud, where it freezes to form a hailstone. This small hailstone can start to fall and be carried up again, having another layer of ice added to it. In this way, hailstones can become larger and larger, sometimes reaching the size of golf balls. Large hailstones can break glass and damage cars. Luckily, most hailstones rarely exceed the size of peas.

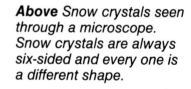

Above Snow crystals seen through a microscope. Snow crystals are always six-sided and every one is a different shape.

Left Wet, melting snow is just right for making snowballs.

ACTIVITY

THE SHAPE OF A SNOW CRYSTAL

YOU NEED

- **a saucer**
- **white paper**
- **scissors**

1 Put the saucer onto the sheet of paper. Draw around the saucer.

2 Remove the saucer and cut out the circle of white paper.

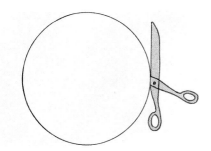

3 Fold the circle in half.

4 Fold the half-circle into thirds by bending one segment over to match another segment. Fold it inward.

5 Fold the other segment inward.

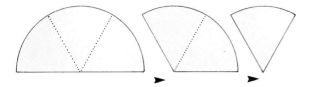

6 Open out your circle and check that the segments are equal. Cut halfway along each fold from the outside inward.

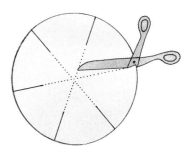

7 Fold the paper up again, then fold it over once more.

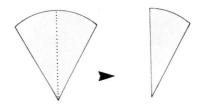

8 Cut the corners off the folded paper.

9 Cut pieces out of the straight sides.

10 Open out your paper. You have made a snow crystal shape. Make other paper snow crystals.

TEST YOURSELF

1. Draw the pattern of a snow crystal.
2. Describe how snowflakes are formed.
3. How are hailstones made?

THE WATER CYCLE

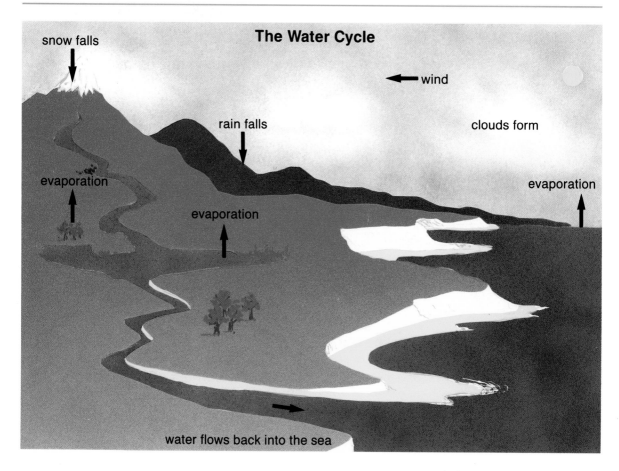

The Water Cycle

snow falls

wind

rain falls

clouds form

evaporation

evaporation

evaporation

water flows back into the sea

Every plant and animal needs water in order to survive. The water cycle provides the Earth with a continual supply of water.

About two-thirds of the Earth's surface is covered by oceans. The sun's rays heat the oceans and cause some of the water to evaporate into water vapor, much of which condenses and forms clouds (see page 22). Clouds that form over oceans often shed rain that falls back into the oceans, but some clouds are blown over land.

The sun's rays also heat up the land and evaporate water from lakes, rivers, and streams. When animals and humans breathe, they put water vapor into the air. You can see the effect of this when you exhale on a cold, clear day. Your breath forms a cloud because the warm, moist air you breathe out is cooled below its dew point (see page 20). Plants draw in water from the soil through their roots. Later this water evaporates from their leaves.

The water cycle is completed when water evaporated from land and sea condenses and falls back to Earth as precipitation (rain, snow, and hail). This precipitation returns the water to the oceans, lakes, rivers, soil, and eventually, to the plants and animals. This process happens continually. Because of air currents and weather patterns, water evaporated from one place usually falls somewhere far away.

ACTIVITY

MEASURING THE HUMIDITY OF THE AIR

YOU NEED

- **2 thermometers**
- **large cotton balls**
- **2 rubber bands**
- **water**
- **a plastic tub**
- **a dry, sunny day**

1 Wrap the bulb of each thermometer in the same amount of cotton.
2 Use rubber bands to hold the cotton to the thermometers.
3 Gently pull the end of the cotton into a point.
4 Soak the cotton on one thermometer with water. Leave the other thermometer dry.
5 Put water in the plastic tub. Place it under the wet thermometer to keep the cotton wet.

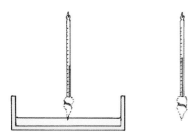

6 Hang both thermometers outside in the shade for 30 minutes.

7 Read the temperatures of both thermometers. Notice that the wet thermometer registers a cooler temperature than the dry thermometer.
8 Record both temperatures.
9 Work out the difference in temperature between the thermometers.

Wet thermometer (°F)	
Dry thermometer (°F)	
Difference between wet and dry thermometers (°F)	

10 Use the chart below to calculate the humidity of the air.

Humidity chart

		Dry temperature		
		50-57°F	59-66°F	68-77°F
Difference between wet and dry thermometers	34°F	85%	90%	90%
	36°F	75%	80%	80%
	38°F	60%	65%	70%
	39°F	50%	60%	65%
	41°F	40%	50%	55%
	43°F	30%	40%	45%
	45°F	15%	30%	40%
	46°F	5%	20%	30%
	48°F	0%	10%	25%
	50°F	0%	5%	20%

11 Repeat your recordings at different times of day.

TEST YOURSELF

1. Describe the water cycle. Draw a picture to help you.
2. What is the energy that drives the water cycle?
3. Why is the water cycle so important?

LIGHTS IN THE SKY

There are many different light effects in the sky. They usually depend on the weather. Here are some that you will probably have seen.

Rainbows are caused by sunlight striking falling raindrops. A sun ray strikes the top or bottom of a raindrop and the light is bent inward, toward the middle of the drop. It is then reflected off the back of the raindrop and the light is bent again as the ray leaves the drop. White light, such as sunlight, is made up of the colors of the spectrum. There are seven main colors: red, orange, yellow, green, blue, indigo, and violet. The bending light separates the colors, forming a rainbow.

Sun halos are similar, but here, the sun's rays are passing through ice crystals, like those found in cirrus clouds. The tiny crystals act like cut diamonds, bending the light and then reflecting it.

Lightning is caused by violent air currents inside a cumulonimbus cloud. These air currents rub the water drops, hailstones, or ice crystals together and the cloud is charged with static electricity. Positive charges collect at the top of the cloud and negative charges at the bottom. The charges build up so much that the negative charge jumps. The charge can jump inside the cloud, giving sheet lightning, or down to the ground, giving forked lightning.

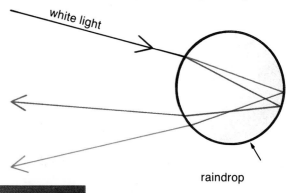

white light

raindrop

Above *When white light from the sun strikes a raindrop, the light is split into the colors of the spectrum (red, orange, yellow, green, blue, indigo, and violet). In the diagram, only red and violet light are shown; the other colors lie between them, in order.*

Left *The moon can sometimes appear to have a halo, when light passes through ice crystals in very high clouds.*

ACTIVITY

MAKING A RAINBOW

> ### YOU NEED
>
> - **a clean drinking glass**
> - **water**
> - **sunshine**
> - **a large sheet of paper**
> - **paints**

1 Stand a glass full of water on a window sill in bright sunlight.

2 Place the sheet of paper on the floor below the window sill.
3 Move the glass until you see the rainbow on the paper.

4 Identify the colors of the rainbow. Paint these colors in a picture.

5 Next time you see a weather rainbow, look to see where the sun and clouds are. Sometimes you can see a double rainbow. This is a normal rainbow, with another, paler rainbow outside it, with the colors in reverse order.

Rainbows can often be seen if the sun shines while it is still raining. To see a rainbow clearly, stand with your back to the sun and look toward the falling raindrops.

> ## TEST YOURSELF
>
> **1.** How are rainbows made?
> **2.** What are sun halos and how are they caused?
> **3.** How is lightning caused?

AIR PRESSURE AND AIR MASSES

Over 300 years ago the Italian scientist Evangelista Torricelli discovered that the air presses on everything. He invented the barometer to measure air pressure. At sea level, the pressure is about 14.7 pounds per square inch. This is the same as having a 14.7-pound weight standing on one square inch of ground. The air pressure falls as you get higher above the Earth's surface. At about 16,500 ft, the air pressure is about half its value at sea level. This is because there are fewer air particles to cause pressure.

Dry air has high pressure, but air saturated with water vapor has a lower pressure. This is because the water vapor takes up space, forcing the air particles apart, so there is less air there to create pressure.

Air pressure enables us to study air masses. These huge areas of air are named after the kind of climate they come from. If the air mass is over the sea it is called maritime. If the air mass is over land, it is called continental.

There are four main types of air mass in the world. Tropical continental is warm, dry, high-pressure. Tropical maritime is warm, moist, low-pressure. Polar continental is cold, dry, high-pressure. Polar maritime is cold and fairly moist, low-pressure. These air masses are moved by the world wind patterns.

Above A weather balloon (see page 40) like this one at a weather station in Colorado can be sent up 18 mi. into the stratosphere to record air-pressure changes.

Right Many people have a barometer in their home. Most barometers give a reading in millibars (mb).

ACTIVITY

AIR PRESSURE

1 Read the air pressure with your barometer.

2 Take the air pressure reading every 3 hours, until the air pressure changes. Is the air pressure rising or falling? What is happening to the weather?

Time	Air pressure	Weather summary
9:00		
12:00		
3:00		

3 Look at some weather maps. Places with the same air pressure are joined by a line called an isobar.

4 Find where you live on a weather map. What is the air pressure in the area where you live?

5 Which other places have the same pressure? Which places are showing a higher or lower pressure?

6 Find a low-pressure area. What is the lowest pressure? Notice that the pressure goes down in the middle of this area.

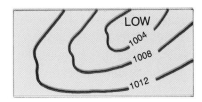

7 Find a high-pressure area. Where is the highest pressure area? Notice that the pressure goes up in the middle. The closer the isobars, the greater the wind speed.

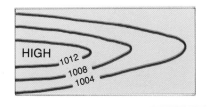

In the northern hemisphere, winds blow clockwise around a high-pressure region and counterclockwise around a low-pressure region. In the southern hemisphere, winds blow clockwise around a low-pressure area and counterclockwise around a high-pressure area.

TEST YOURSELF

1. Which instrument do you use to measure air pressure?
2. Which gives the higher pressure—wet air or dry air?
3. Describe the four main types of air mass.

A WARM FRONT

A front is the dividing line between the warm, moist air of a cyclone, or depression (area of low pressure), and the cold, dry air of an anticyclone (area of high pressure). The leading edge of a depression is called the warm front.

When two large air masses meet, moving in opposite directions, the warm, moist air mass rises above the denser, dry air mass. As it rises the water vapor condenses, forming a series of different cloud types. The clouds become lower and thicker, bringing rain.

Below *This diagram shows four towns, 180 mi. apart, in the path of a warm front.*

Warm front

warm air

cold air

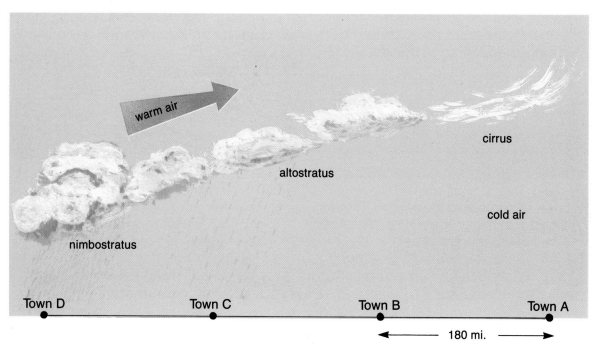

warm air

cirrus

altostratus

cold air

nimbostratus

Town D   Town C   Town B   Town A

180 mi.

Town A has clear, cold weather, with a few high cirrus clouds. Town B has thicker, lower clouds and the sky is gray. Town C has dark altostratus clouds and a light drizzle.

Town D has nimbostratus clouds with heavy rain. When it stops it will be warm and humid. It takes about 12 hours for weather to get from one town to the next.

ACTIVITY

SEARCHING FOR DEPRESSIONS

YOU NEED

- **weather maps from newspapers, for several days in a row**
- **a ruler**

Below *Weather forecasting is especially important for safety at sea and for people enjoying leisure activities like this yachting event off New Zealand.*

1 Find a depression on the map. Where is its leading edge?
2 Look at the cities that the depression covers, from the front edge to the center of the depression.
3 Predict the weather for each city (see page 34).
4 Look at the weather reports for these cities for several days. Does your prediction match the experts?
5 Look at the weather maps for several days. How does the weather change? Do the weather reports match the air-pressure charts?

TEST YOURSELF

1. Where do you find warm fronts?
2. How are warm fronts formed?
3. Predict the weather that is likely to occur as a warm front passes.

A COLD FRONT

Two fronts are formed around a depression—a warm front ahead of it and a cold front behind it. The cold front marks the edge of approaching cold air. As the cold air moves forward, it forces itself under the warm air like a huge wedge. As this happens, the water vapor in the warm front rises and condenses even faster. This sudden cooling creates towering cumulonimbus thunderclouds. The weather will become stormy. Rain will continue as the front passes, then the barometer will rise. Gradually, bright, clear air will move forward as the clouds get thinner.

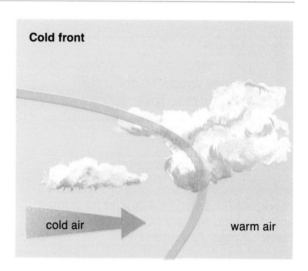

Below *These four towns, 125 miles apart, are in the path of a cold front.*

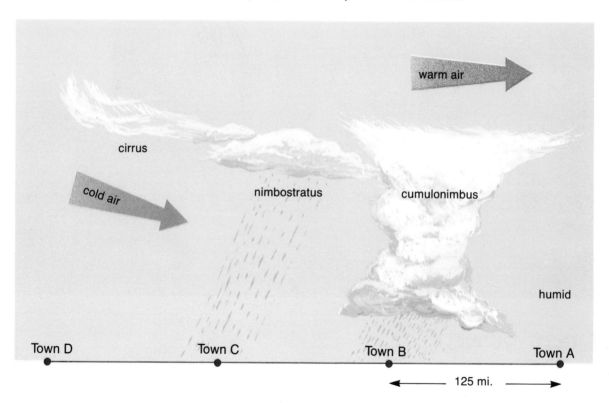

Town A has warm, moist air. Town B has large cumulonimbus clouds, thunderstorms and torrential rain. Town C has rain from nimbostratus clouds. Town D has bright, cool air.

ACTIVITY

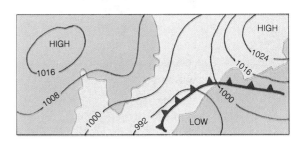

YOU NEED

- **weather maps from newspapers for several days (that include anticyclones)**
- **a ruler**

1 Where is the cold front on the map?
2 Which towns are under that leading edge?

3 What is the forecast for those towns?
4 Notice that high-pressure areas tend to be larger than low-pressure areas (see page 33).

The temperature outside does not always tell you how cold it feels. The speed of the wind makes a difference. It creates the wind-chill factor. If the wind blows hard, the temperature feels colder than the thermometer reading.

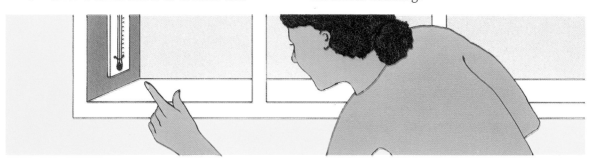

Wind chill chart	Outside temperature						
Wind speed (mph)	44° F	39° F	35.5°F	34° F	25° F	19.5°F	
5	43° F	37.5°F	32° F	26.5°F	21° F	16° F	
10	34° F	28.5°F	21° F	17.5°F	10.5°F	3.2°F	
15	28.5°F	23° F	16° F	8.5°F	2.2°F	- 6° F	Wind
20	26.5°F	19.5°F	12.2°F	3.2°F	2.2°F	- 9.5°F	chill
25	23° F	16° F	8.5°F	1.5°F	- 7.5°F	-15° F	temperature
30	21° F	12.2°F	7° F	- 2.2°F	- 9.5°F	-18.5°F	
35	19.5°F	12.2°F	3.2°F	- 4° F	-11.2°F	-20.2°F	

TEST YOURSELF

1. What is a cold front?
2. What weather would you expect to get as a cold front passes?
3. Draw a weather map with isobars, an anticyclone, and a cold front.

JET STREAMS AND HURRICANES

Between 6 and 7 miles above the Earth's surface, a wind blows, like a river of air. This is called the jet stream. There is a westerly jet stream in the northern and in the southern hemispheres, blowing toward the east. Both jet streams blow continuously, right around the world, between latitudes 40° and 70°. The northern jet stream is called the polar front jet stream. The wind in these jet streams blows at speeds from 60 mph to over 180 mph. Aircraft flying eastward try to fly in the jet stream, in order to be carried along by it.

A hurricane is a severe storm. In China and Japan, it is called a typhoon. In India, it is called a cyclone, and in Australia, a willy-willy. Hurricanes occur over tropical seas and develop as deep depressions. They spin counterclockwise in the northern hemisphere and clockwise in the southern hemisphere.

A hurricane with warmth and moisture in it will grow bigger and stronger, measuring up to 1,200 mi. across. The wind speed may reach 180 mph. The low-pressure center is known as the eye of the storm. Here, the air is quite calm, compared to its surroundings. This can be very deceiving.

If the storm strikes land, great damage is done on the coast. As the hurricane moves inland, it is without moisture from the sea. It slowly dies, the winds slacken, and the eye fills in.

Tornadoes are small but powerful whirlwinds that may form suddenly within severe storms. Wind speeds may reach up to 300 mph, higher than any hurricane.

Above Satellites (see page 40) are able to send back clear pictures of weather. This one is Hurricane Pat over the Western Pacific.

Left A tornado may only last a few minutes but it is immensely powerful and can cause a great deal of damage. The whirling funnel of wind hangs from the bottom of a cumulonimbus cloud like a length of hose.

ACTIVITIES

JET STREAMS

> **YOU NEED**
>
> - **an airline timetable**
> - **a globe or atlas of the world**

1 Use your timetable to find out the flight time of an aircraft going from Chicago to London.
2 Compare this with the time taken for the aircraft to travel from London to Chicago.
3 Remember to allow for the difference between Chicago and London local times. (An atlas will have a world map showing time zones.)
4 Check the times of aircraft to and from Honolulu and Chicago; to and from Athens and Chicago. Remember to allow for time zones.
5 What do you notice about the times to and from these places?
6 Look at your globe or atlas. What is the general direction of each place from Chicago?
7 What is the effect of the jet stream?
8 Try other flight times that you think will be affected by the jet stream.

HURRICANES

> **YOU NEED**
>
> - **newspaper reports about hurricanes**

1 Display the hurricane reports.
2 Record when and where they occurred. What was the maximum wind speed recorded? How much damage was done? Find out all you can about each storm.

Right In 1988, Hurricane Gilbert hit Jamaica and overturned this plane.

TEST YOURSELF

1. What is the jet stream?
2. What are hurricanes and what makes them grow stronger?
3. What happens to hurricanes when they reach land?

FORECASTING THE WEATHER

In order to forecast what the weather will be like tomorrow, it is essential to know, in as much detail as possible, what the weather is like today.

People on the move need to know what kind of weather they will meet on their trips. For this reason, there are weather reports for commuters, the police, ships at sea, and airlines. Ships' captains and airline pilots spend a lot of time arranging their routes to take advantage of the weather. Farmers, power-supply engineers, and road-maintenance workers all need accurate weather information.

In order to obtain all this information, weather satellites orbit the Earth, sending down information and pictures every 30 minutes. Free-flying balloons are sent to heights of up to 18 miles above the Earth. They transmit information about temperature, air-pressure, and humidity. The balloons are tracked to record how they move in the winds of the stratosphere. Weather ships and weather stations on land send in detailed weather maps and reports every six hours to meteorological centers.

Modern weather forecasting relies on computers not only to analyze the information from hundreds of weather stations but also to highlight changes and trends. This enables the forecaster to predict future weather patterns.

Left *TIROS weather satellites orbit the Earth and send back weather information at 2-hour intervals. TIROS stands for Television Infra-Red Orbital Satellite.*

ACTIVITY

1 Look at a TV weather forecast.
2 What weather systems are illustrated?
3 What frontal systems are shown?
4 In which direction are these systems moving?
5 What forecast was given by the forecaster?
6 What reasons were given for this forecast?
7 Which symbols were used?
8 Look at newspaper weather reports. What weather systems are shown?
9 Which weather symbols are used? What forecasts are given?
10 What is the weather like today? What type of weather would you expect tomorrow?
11 Draw a large weather map showing weather systems and symbols.

12 Display this map and give a weather forecast to your friends, pretending to be a forecaster.

6pm Today

Above *A weather forecaster shows us current weather patterns and gives us tomorrow's forecast.*

Below *Some examples of weather symbols. They may vary in different newspapers and on different television channels.*

cloudy - fine weather   rain   snow   (15) temperature (°F)

AIR POLLUTION

You have probably read or heard a great deal about air pollution. There are many ways that humans cause pollution. Politicians, scientists, and the general public are worried about the effects of this. We use large amounts of fossil fuels (gas, oil, and coal) for a number of purposes. These fuels are used for heating, to produce electricity, in industry, and by cars, trucks, trains, and aircraft. When these fuels are burned, gases—mainly carbon dioxide, sulfur dioxide, and oxides of nitrogen—are produced.

Acid rain is one seriously damaging result. The gases sulfur dioxide and oxides of nitrogen combine with water droplets in the air to form acid. When these droplets condense, they fall as acid rain. This can kill plants and life in rivers and lakes.

Certain chemicals released into the atmosphere can break down the special oxygen compound in the ozone layer. Ozone usually forms a protective blanket around the world, blocking out many of the harmful rays from the sun. Where holes form in the ozone layer more harmful rays can reach the Earth's surface and damage living things.

Below *The purple patches in these satellite pictures show the growing hole in the ozone layer over the South Pole.*

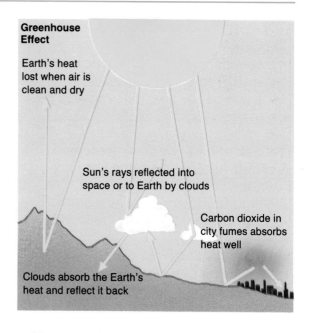

Greenhouse Effect

Earth's heat lost when air is clean and dry

Sun's rays reflected into space or to Earth by clouds

Carbon dioxide in city fumes absorbs heat well

Clouds absorb the Earth's heat and reflect it back

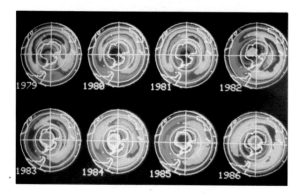

You may also know about the greenhouse effect. There are several pollutants that cause this, but the most important is carbon dioxide. Green plants take in carbon dioxide and give out oxygen. Animals do the opposite, and ideally there should be a balance. However, as vast areas of forest are cut down and cleared, and fossil fuels are burned in large amounts, the level of carbon dioxide rises all over the world. This gas forms a layer in the atmosphere. The sun's energy can penetrate this layer, but gets trapped under it, just as it would by the glass in a greenhouse. This causes the overall world temperature to rise. Living things that are sensitive to temperature changes could suffer seriously as a result. The extra heat could also melt the polar icecaps, causing flooding, as well as other harmful changes in weather patterns.

People all over the world are trying to improve the situation, but, unfortunately, it is very expensive to stop the major pollutants from entering the atmosphere.

ACTIVITY

ACID RAIN

1 Tear the red cabbage leaves into small pieces. Put the cabbage pieces in a bowl.

2 Boil water and pour it on the leaves until they are covered.

3 Carefully use the wooden spoon to squeeze the juice from the leaves into the hot water.

4 Let the cabbage stand for one hour.

5 Use the graduated cylinder to pour 1 oz of distilled water into one jar and 1 oz of rainwater into the other jar.

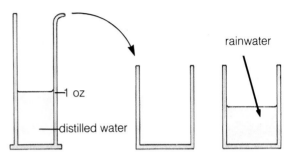

rainwater

1 oz

distilled water

6 Add an equal amount of the purple cabbage juice to each jar. Watch for any change of color.

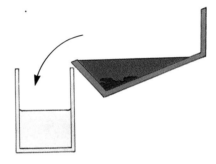

7 Compare the color of the distilled water and the rainwater. If your rainwater turns red, it is acid.

WARNING: Take care when using boiling water. Ask an adult to help you.

TEST YOURSELF

1. What causes acid rain?
2. How is the gas carbon dioxide usually kept constant, or in balance, in our atmosphere?
3. What is the greenhouse effect?

CLIMATE AND AGRICULTURE

The world's population is constantly increasing. In the year 1600 there were only 500 million people in the world. By 1950, this had risen to 2.5 billion. The numbers rise daily, and by the year 2000 the population will probably be over 6 billion.

All these people have to be fed and housed. In order to do this, the world's forests are being cut down to provide land for agriculture, and wood for fuel and building. The forests are also cleared so that land can be mined, or roads, pipelines, power lines, and dams can be built.

Cutting down the forests can seriously affect world weather. The leaves of forest trees release large amounts of moisture into the atmosphere — without them the local rainfall is reduced, which may result in droughts. The trees also take in large quantities of carbon dioxide, helping to lessen the greenhouse effect (see page 42).

Forest trees have deep roots that hold the soil in place and prevent soil erosion. If trees are cut down on hillsides the exposed soil may be washed away by heavy rains, causing disastrous mudslides, the silting up of rivers, and possible flooding. When large areas of cleared forest land are plowed up for crops, winds often blow away the topsoil, creating dust storms. Many of the world's deserts are expanding rapidly, due to weather erosion.

World temperatures today are at their highest recorded level and are continuing to rise. Partly caused by the greenhouse effect, this global warming will seriously affect farming and food production. Lowlying agricultural land will flood if the sea level rises, while elsewhere good agricultural land will suffer more frequent droughts. As climatic zones shift, so too will the world's major agricultural regions.

An area of rain forest being cleared in Brazil. Over 40 percent of the world's rain forests have already been destroyed.

ACTIVITY

1 Use the information from conservation organizations to see where the world's forests are being cut down.
2 Why are these forests being cut?

3 What is the predicted effect on the climate locally and worldwide?
4 Where in the world are forests being planted?
5 Read reports on the spread of deserts and weather disasters, such as drought, dust storms, river flooding, and mudslides.
6 Find out about local conservation projects. Where are trees used as a windbreak? Is there evidence of soil erosion? Where are woodland areas being destroyed or planted?
7 Look at old maps. How has the ground changed over the years?
8 Write reports of your findings. Display them as an exhibition.

Serious droughts, like this one in New South Wales, Australia, can lead to the death of livestock.

Global warming has already caused the sea level to rise, leading to more frequent floods in lowland regions.

TEST YOURSELF

1. How do you think the increase in world population affects the climate?
2. What causes the spread of deserts?
3. What changes have occurred in your area that you think could have some effect on your local climate?

Glossary

Anemometer An instrument for measuring wind speed.

Anticyclone A high-pressure weather system.

Atmosphere The layer of air around the Earth.

Axis An imaginary line about which a given body or system rotates.

Barometer An instrument for measuring atmospheric pressure.

Climate The average weather conditions at any place recorded for a time.

Condense To turn a gas into a liquid. For example, water vapor is turned into water by cooling.

Convection current A rising current of air caused by heating. Rising warm air is replaced by cold air, and is heated and rises. The warm air cools and falls.

Depression A low-pressure weather system. Also called a **cyclone**.

Dew point The temperature at which water vapor in the air condenses into droplets of liquid water.

Drizzle Very fine rain, consisting of drops less than 0.02 inches in diameter.

Drought A serious shortage of water.

Erosion The wearing down of land by the action of wind and water that gradually removes soil or rocks.

Evaporate To change a liquid into a gas. For example, water changes to water vapor when heated.

Front The boundary that separates two large air masses.

Humidity A measure of the amount of water in the air; given as a percentage.

Meteorological center A place where weather forecasts are made from weather information.

Pollution Anything that spoils the environment. Usually, chemicals that foul the air, land, rivers, and oceans.

Precipitation The name for any condensation falling from clouds.

Reflection Light bouncing off a surface.

Satellite A small object moving around a larger one, such as the moon around the Earth. Weather satellites are constructed and launched by humans.

Saturate To fill completely. When air is saturated, its humidity is 100 percent and it will not absorb any more water.

Solstice The time of the year when the sun reaches its point of farthest distance north or south of the equator.

Static electricity A build-up of electrical charge, usually caused by friction.

Supercooled When a liquid is cooled below its normal freezing point, but has not become solid.

Temperate The climatic zone between the polar regions and the tropics. Neither very hot nor very cold.

Thunder The rumble of thunder is actually a "sonic boom" caused by the rapid expansion of the air around an intensely hot flash of lightning.

Trade winds Tropical winds that blow toward the equator.

Tropics Hot regions of the Earth on both sides of the equator, between the Tropics of Cancer and Capricorn.

Vapor A gas.

Water table The underground water level; the surface of the water-saturated part of the ground.

Westerlies Temperate winds that blow away from the tropics toward the temperate latitudes.

Books to Read

Conserving the Atmosphere, John Baines
(Steck-Vaughn, 1989)
Weather, Martyn Bramwell (Franklin Watts, 1988)
Weather, Mark Pettigrew (Franklin Watts, 1987)
Weather and Its Work, David Lambert & Ralph Hardy (Facts on File, 1985)

Picture Acknowledgments

The author and publishers would like to thank the following for allowing illustrations to be reproduced in this book: Chapel Studios 32 (right); Chris Fairclough Colour Library *frontispiece*, 16; Hutchison Library 45 (right); A. & M. Meinel 30; Liz Miller 31; NASA 42; TOPHAM 38 (above), 39; Wayland Picture Library 7 (Chris Fairclough), 35, 41, 45 (left/David Bowden); ZEFA *cover*, 6, 12, 18, 20, 22, 23, 24, 26, 32 (left), 38 (left), 40, 44. Cover artwork by Marilyn Clay. All other artwork by Jenny Hughes.

Index

551.4   Catherall, Ed
Cat
         Exploring weather

Anderson Elementary